THE PRINCIPLES AND
POWER OF
VISION

STUDY
GUIDE

THE PRINCIPLES AND POWER OF VISION

STUDY GUIDE

DR. MYLES MUNROE

WHITAKER
HOUSE

THE PRINCIPLES AND POWER OF VISION STUDY GUIDE
workbook edition

Munroe Global
P.O. Box N9583
Nassau, Bahamas
www.munroeglobal.com
office@munroeglobal.com

ISBN: 978-0-88368-389-7
eBook ISBN: 978-1-60374-782-0
Printed in the United States of America
© 2003 by Munroe Group of Companies Ltd.

Whitaker House
1030 Hunt Valley Circle
New Kensington, PA 15068
www.whitakerhouse.com

The Library of Congress has cataloged the trade paperback edition as follows:

Munroe, Myles.
  The principles and power of vision. Study guide / Myles Munroe.
      p.   cm.
  ISBN 0-88368-953-7 (pbk.)
  1. Vocation—Christianity.   2. Success—Religious aspects—Christianity.
3. Self-realization—Religious aspects—Christianity.   I. Title.
  BV4740.M84 2003
  248.4—dc22

                          2003015620

6 7 8 9 10 11 12 13 14 15 16 **UJ** 29 28 27 26 25 24 23 22

Contents

How to Use This Study Guide

This study guide complement to *The Principles and Power of Vision* by Dr. Myles Munroe may be used by either individuals or groups and can be easily adapted to suit the needs of both. For your convenience, an answer key is provided in the back of this study guide.

Each chapter review includes the following elements:

Chapter Theme: The main idea of each chapter is summarized for emphasis and clarity.

Questions for Reflection: One or more questions are given as a warm-up to lead into the study or discussion of the topic. (For group study, these questions may be asked before or after reading the Chapter Theme, at the leader's discretion.)

Exploring Principles and Purposes: Questions and review material are provided to highlight and summarize the truths and principles within each chapter and begin to lead the reader/group participant to personalize what is being studied. Page numbers corresponding to the book are listed for easy reference.

Conclusion: A summary or implication statement is included to put the chapter theme into perspective.

Applying the Principles of Vision: Thought-provoking questions and suggestions for personal action and prayer are provided to help the individual/group participant apply the study material to his or her particular life circumstances. This section includes three parts:

- Thinking It Over
- Acting on It
- Praying about It

One of the most important things we can find out about ourselves is the purpose of our existence. As you progress through *The Principles and Power of Vision* and review its truths and practical applications through this study guide, you will come to understand your personal purpose and potential and discover how to recognize and fulfill your life's vision.

Introduction

No matter who you are or what country you live in, you have a personal purpose, for every human being is born with one. God created each person with a unique vision. He has tremendous plans for you that no one else can accomplish. The tragic thing is that many people live their whole lives without ever recognizing their visions. A lack of purpose and unfulfilled potential is epidemic in our world. I travel to many nations speaking to various groups, and I meet people on every continent who have no sense of personal, corporate, or national purpose. I see them struggling with aimless or misdirected lives.

Most people's lives do not reflect who they truly are or what they can be. Inside them are dreams that are not yet reality, gifts and talents they have not yet developed, purposes for their lives that are not yet fulfilled, the "something" they've always wanted to be or do but for some reason have not been able to accomplish. I wrote *The Principles and Power of Vision* (the result of thirty years of my research into purpose and potential) to show you how to discover, develop, and fulfill your personal vision. Now, this study guide companion will help you capture your vision and put it into practice even more fully in your life.

Vision is a conception that is inspired by God in the heart of a human. The greatest gift God ever gave humanity is not sight, but vision. Sight is a function of the eyes, but vision is a function of the heart. You can have sight but no vision. Throughout history, progress has been made only by people who have "seen" things that were not yet here. Vision is seeing the future before it comes into being. It is a mental picture of your destiny. God gave humanity the gift of vision so we would not have to live only by what we see.

What have you always wanted to do? What is your heart's desire? What is your dream? When you can begin to see your vision clearly, you will be able to fulfill your life's purpose. The essence of vision is the ability to see farther than your physical eyes can look—to see not just what is, but also what can be and to make it a reality.

Consider this analogy: The destiny of an acorn is a tree. By faith, you can see the tree within the seed. You have a vision of it in your mind's eye because you know the potential in the seed. The same thing is true for you and me. God has given us birth for a purpose, and as far as God is concerned, that purpose is already finished because He has placed within us the potential for fulfilling it. We can see that purpose through faith. To paraphrase the Bible, faith is the substance of things you hope to accomplish, the evidence of things you can see even when others cannot. Only by seeing what is not yet here can you bring something new, creative, and exciting into existence. Your dreams, talents, and desires can be refined in a process of discovering and fulfilling your vision so that your unique and personal gifts to this world will shine forth.

I believe with all my heart that when you have no vision, you will simply relive the past with its disappointments and failures. As long as a person has vision, however, there is always a chance for him to move out of his present circumstances and toward the fulfillment of his purpose. Therefore, vision is the key to your future. This study guide will help you to reassess your life's strategies and make the necessary adjustments so you can plan for the future and not make the same mistakes and decisions that have hindered you in the past. You will come to understand the principles of vision as well as the practical tools and skills necessary to bring your vision into reality.

—Myles Munroe

Chapter One

VISION: The Key to Fulfilling Your Life's Purpose

GOD HAS PLACED WITHIN EACH PERSON A VISION THAT IS
DESIGNED TO GIVE PURPOSE AND MEANING TO LIFE.

CHAPTER THEME

One of the dilemmas of contemporary society is a lack of meaningfulness and purpose in everyday life. If you ask people, "Why do you exist?" most cannot tell you. They can't explain their purpose in the world. Many people are also struggling with job and life satisfaction issues.

Some people are fairly content with their lives, but they have a vague sense that there should be more significance to life than they are experiencing. Still others live on a surface level, pursuing a series of emotional highs that leave them empty and constantly searching for the next thrill that might satisfy them.

Do you have a sense of personal purpose? Do you know why you were born? Does your purpose give you a passion for living? You *can* know why you exist, fulfill your God-given purpose, and experience a remarkable life in light of that knowledge. Hidden within you is the key to living a more fulfilling life than you ever imagined. That key is *vision*.

Questions for Reflection

1. Are you satisfied with your life/job? What do you especially like or not like about it? How do you wish it were different?

2. Do you feel that you are fulfilling your potential in life? Why or why not?

Exploring Principles and Purposes

3. The poorest person in the world is a person without a _____. (p. 24)

4. What can happen when people have no vision beyond their current circumstances? (p. 24)

5. Although people often have all kinds of ideas in their minds, what pattern usually occurs in relation to these ideas? (pp. 25–26)

6. While the poorest person in the world is a person without a dream, the most *frustrated* person in the world is someone who _____ _____ _____. (p. 26)

7. What are some reasons why a person will abandon or get sidetracked from his or her dream? (p. 26)

8. God not only created each person on earth with a distinct _____, but He also placed in everyone a unique _____. (p. 28)

9. Fulfilling our visions or dreams brings what to our lives? (p. 28)

10. How did Dr. Munroe define "the very substance of life"? (p. 28)

11. What was every human being created to accomplish? (p. 28)

12. You were designed to be _____ for something _____. (pp. 28–29)

13. One person with vision is greater than _____ _____. (p. 31)

14. What will make a way for you in the world and enable you to fulfill your vision? (pp. 32–33)

15. Why did Dr. Munroe say that education, in itself, is not the key to success? (p. 33)

16. While the gift is in you, what responsibility do you have in regard to it? (p. 34) In what ways can you do this? (p. 34)

17. What role does education have in relation to your gift? (p. 34)

18. Although we are all born as _____, most of us become _____. (p. 35) How can you prevent this from happening to you? (pp. 35–36)

19. Circle one: True or False

    By a certain age, we are too old to use our gifts. (p. 36)

20. How can a person realize his dream and not let that dream become a nightmare of unfulfilled hopes? (p. 37)

21. Your success in life depends on— [choose one] (pp. 37–38)

    (a) the state of the economy.

    (b) what careers are currently in demand.

    (c) what the job market is like.

    (d) your initial resources.

    (e) what other people think you are capable of.

    (f) your understanding and practicing the principles of vision.

22. In terms of fulfilling our visions, what are we the sum total of? (p. 38)

23. God has given you the _____ and the _____ to achieve your life's vision. (p. 38)

Conclusion

Every person has been given a vision for life, as well as one or more gifts that will enable him to fulfill that vision. Most people do things because they *have* to. Vision enables you to do things because you have *decided* to, based on your purpose. You were created to accomplish something that no one else can accomplish. Dream big. Somewhere inside you there is always the ability to dream. No matter how challenging it gets, don't give up, because your vision is the key to fulfilling your life's purpose.

Applying the Principles of Vision

Thinking It Over

- Do you know the answer to the question, "Why do you exist?" If so, what is the reason for your existence? If not, begin to write down any thoughts you have regarding your purpose; keep refining them as you progress through this book.

- How successful have you been in achieving your goals? What is helping you/hindering you in achieving them?

- Before reading this chapter, which of the following statements best described your overall goal in life: "I am retired" or "It is finished" (I have finished the purpose for which I was created)? Has your goal changed since reading this chapter? Why or why not?

Acting on It

- Make a list of your unique gifts, personal qualities, and interests. Then note whether or not there is a strong connection between these gifts, personal qualities, and interests and the primary work and activities you are involved in.

- Write down ways you can develop, refine, and use your gifts.

Praying about It

- Ask God to help you see the vision He has placed inside you.

- Give thanks to God for the particular gifts and abilities He has given you.

- Read and mediate on this Scripture to remind yourself that God has created you with both a distinct design and a distinct purpose:

For you created my inmost being; you knit me together in my mother's womb. I praise you because I am fearfully and wonderfully made; your works are wonderful, I know that full well. (Psalm 139:13–14)

YOUR PURPOSE WILL BECOME YOUR PASSION.

NOTES

Chapter Two
The Source of Vision

VISION IS FORESIGHT WITH INSIGHT BASED ON HINDSIGHT.

CHAPTER THEME

The first step to fulfilling your reason for existence was realizing that you have been given a vision. Yet how exactly do you receive, recognize, and activate your vision? When you understand the source of vision, you will learn the secrets to its origin and working in your life. This knowledge will help you to take your dream from initial idea all the way to fulfillment.

Question for Reflection

1. Why or how did you become involved with your job, major hobbies, and other important activities in your life? (In other words, what was your motivation for or the circumstances surrounding your choices?)

Exploring Principles and Purposes

2. What does vision always emanate from? Why is this so? (p. 41)

3. God has given you a special purpose to _____. (p. 42)

4. You were born at the _____ _____ to accomplish your vision during your _____. (p. 43)

5. How is the vision in your heart "a piece of eternity"? (pp. 43–44)

6. In what sense is your purpose already completed? (pp. 44–46)

7. How should the fact that God always accomplishes His purposes affect the way you carry out your vision? (p. 46)

8. What is the difference between recognizing your purpose and having a vision? (p. 47)

9. At its essence, what is vision about? Why? (p. 48)

10. What is the key to recognizing personal vision? (pp. 48–49)

11. Why do we have thoughts that keep coming back to us and desires that never leave us throughout our lives? (p. 49)

12. What is one way to discern whether or not something is a vision from God? (p. 51)

13. What is a second way to recognize true vision? (p. 51)

14. A third way to know a genuine vision is that true vision is _____. (p. 51) In light of this quality, what does a real vision focus on? (p. 51)

15. Name two things that indicate a person is pursuing selfish interests rather than true vision. (pp. 52–53)

16. Vision should always be accompanied by _____. (p. 52)

17. What is a fourth way of knowing that a vision is real? (p. 53)

18. Why don't many people recognize the vision God has placed within them? (p. 54)

19. What is a fifth key to understanding true vision? (p. 55)

20. How does the process of this fifth key work? (p. 55)

21. We must have an attitude of _____ with those with whom we share corporate vision. (p. 57)

22. God brings corporate vision into your life in order to— [choose one] (p. 58)
    (a) decrease the importance of your vision.
    (b) give you vision.
    (c) stir up your personal vision.
    (d) frustrate your individual plans.

23. Why are you a leader in the specific purpose God has given you to accomplish through your gift(s)? (pp. 58–59)

24. In what way does vision generate vision? (pp. 59–60)

25. What will help you to keep stirring up your vision? (p. 60)

Conclusion

Many people are waiting for God to tell them what to do in life when it has been given to them already. God has been speaking to them since they were born, and He is still speaking to them now through the thoughts, ideas, and visions they keep having in their minds. Likewise, God planned in advance all that you were born to be and accomplish. Not only does He establish your end, but He also gives you a glimpse of it through the vision He has put in your heart. You are not an experiment. God created you for a purpose, and He will bring that purpose to pass.

Applying the Principles of Vision

Thinking It Over

- Ultimately, our visions aren't about ourselves but about God and His purposes. Has this been your perspective on fulfilling your vision? Why or why not? In what ways has your perspective changed since reading this chapter?

- Dr. Munroe said that others can confirm your vision, but that they do not *give* you your vision. Have you been looking to others to give you a vision rather than to God and the ideas and desires He has put in your heart? If so, what will you do to seek your true vision from now on?

- No great work was ever done by just one person. Yet sometimes people try to fulfill their visions by themselves instead of working with those who share the vision. Are you cooperating with others in the vision in which you are involved? How can you work more harmoniously with them?

Acting on It

- God will reveal your vision as you follow Him, listen to Him, and pay attention to what He has placed in your heart and mind. Have you been listening to what God has been saying? If not, make a point to begin to do so today. To start, take half an hour and allow yourself to dream about what you would like to do in life. What ideas and desires do you have? What have you always wanted to do? Write these things down.

- Look again at the list you made in chapter 1 of your gifts, personal qualities, and interests. In what ways do these fit together with the ideas, dreams, and desires you just wrote down?

- Read over your ideas, desires, and gifts every day for a week. Then ask yourself, "Do these ideas hold true? Are they what I really want to do?" If the answer is yes, keep them where you can refer to them as you read this book, and watch them form into a specific vision and concrete goals that will move you along toward the completion of your purpose. If the answer is no, continually think over and pray about your purpose until your vision becomes clear to you.

Praying about It

- God is committed to your purpose, and He provided salvation through Christ to restore His will in your life and enable you to fulfill your vision. What is your relationship with God? Are you connected to your Source of life and purpose? If not, tell God you want to be restored to Him through the sacrifice of Christ on the cross on your behalf. Then, receive God's forgiveness and commit to living for Him from now on.

- Once we are restored to God, we receive His Holy Spirit and can better see and understand the visions He has placed in our hearts. We also learn to discern true vision through our relationship with God and by reading His Word. Make it a practice to pray and read the Bible every day to help you stay connected to your Source.

- Do you believe that you're not a mistake and that your life is significant? Do you know that your life has a purpose? If you are unclear about your vision, ask God to reveal to you the deepest desires He has placed within you. Then trust Him to help you fulfill your vision.

- Dr. Munroe said that if we pursue visions that we were not meant to pursue, we will not only cause ourselves trouble, but we will also cause others to have problems. If this has been your experience, tell God today that you want to return to Him and what He has purposed for you to do. If you have caused your family members or others turmoil because of selfish pursuits, ask for their forgiveness and seek to restore these relationships.

We are God's workmanship, created in Christ Jesus to do good works, which God prepared in advance for us to do.   (Ephesians 2:10)

PURPOSE IS THE SOURCE OF YOUR VISION.

NOTES

Chapter Three
Overcoming Obstacles to Vision

MEDIOCRITY IS A REGION BORDERED ON THE NORTH BY COMPROMISE, ON THE SOUTH BY
INDECISION, ON THE EAST BY PAST THINKING, AND ON THE WEST BY A LACK OF VISION.
—JOHN MASON

CHAPTER THEME

You must be aware of potential obstacles in your life that can derail your vision so you will be prepared to recognize and overcome them. This chapter will show you how to leave behind fear, doubt, and false perceptions concerning vision so you can successfully pursue and fulfill your life's purpose.

Question for Reflection

1. What do you think is your greatest hindrance to pursuing and/or completing your vision?

Exploring Principles and Purposes

2. Dr. Munroe gave three major obstacles to fulfilling vision. What is the first obstacle? (p. 63)

3. The main thing about vision is that it is _____. (p. 63)

4. Confusing mission with vision can often prevent people from defining a specific vision and fulfilling it. What is the difference between mission and vision? (pp. 64–65)

5. When you have discovered your own vision, you do not need to be _____ of anyone because there's no need for _____. (p. 66)

6. How should we measure the success of our visions? (p. 67)

7. What is a second reason people aren't specific about their visions? (pp. 67–68)

8. We should have _____ rather than mere _____. (p. 68) How can we do this? (p. 68)

9. What is a third reason people's visions never take specific shape? (pp. 68–69)

10. Prolonged indecisiveness about one's life purpose— [choose one] (p. 69)

    (a) is a vision-killer.

    (b) drains the joy out of life.

    (c) makes one's whole life unsettled.

    (d) all of the above

11. Name a fourth reason people do not pursue specific visions. (p. 70)

12. What is a fifth reason people don't focus on specific visions? (p. 70)

13. What does it mean to have true balance in life? (p. 71)

14. A sixth reason people aren't specific about their visions is that they're trying to do what? (p. 71)

15. What important truth set Dr. Munroe free from both indecision and ineffective busyness? (p. 71)

16. You were meant to meet _____ needs, not _____ need. (p. 72)

17. What is a seventh reason some people don't pursue specific visions? (p. 72)

18. If you have many gifts and interests, how can you pursue a specific vision? (p. 73)

_____

_____

_____

_____

19. The first obstacle to fulfilling vision was not recognizing the specific nature of vision. What is the second obstacle? (p. 73)

_____

20. One of the costs of vision is _____. (p. 73)

21. One reason people don't recognize or pay the cost of vision is that they think their lives are out of their own control. What is one way this attitude is manifested? (pp. 73–74)

_____

_____

22. What is a second reason people don't recognize or pay the cost of vision? (p. 74)

_____

23. Name two kinds of outside forces that people blame for the failure of their visions. (p. 74)

_____

_____

24. How do you know that your vision can be fulfilled even though you have made mistakes or experienced setbacks in the past? (pp. 74–75)

_____

_____

25. When the winds of adversity blow in your life, what will be your anchor? (p. 75)

26. What is the third obstacle to accomplishing vision? (p. 75)

27. Successful visionaries don't pursue their visions _____. (p. 75) How *do* successful visionaries operate? (p. 75)

Conclusion

Life was designed to be inspired by purpose and fueled by vision. This means that you don't have to live a defensive life that is made up of crisis management. Instead, you can pursue an offensive life in which you steadily follow your vision and initiate your own goals and actions. The "Twelve Principles for Fulfilling Personal Vision" in the chapters that follow will help you to clarify your vision, formulate a plan for accomplishing it, and bring it to a fulfilling and successful completion as you actively put the principles into practice.

Applying the Principles of Vision

Thinking It Over

- Now that you have completed this chapter, look back at question 1. Do you still think that what you wrote as the answer is your greatest hindrance to pursuing and/or completing your vision? Why or why not? If not, what do you now think is your greatest hindrance? Why?

- Have you been measuring your success by what other people are doing or by what God has called you to do? What will you do to keep focused on your own vision from now on?

- What problems and challenges in life have you allowed to derail your vision? Think about what excuses you might be telling yourself or others for why you aren't pursuing your vision (e.g., "My life is too complicated," "I'm hindered by other people's demands and needs," "I'm not confident enough"). How will you address these excuses based on what you've learned in this chapter?

Acting on It

- Once you have identified your greatest obstacle to achieving your vision, write down specific steps you can take to begin overcoming that obstacle. (For example, have you distinguished between your life's mission and its vision? Will you trust that God is with you and that you are not a victim of "bad luck"? Will you stop blaming others for the way your life has turned out and start thanking God that He will enable you to complete His vision for your life?) Take the first step today.

- If you are indecisive about your vision, first think about why you feel this way: Do you fear failure? Are you worried about what other people might say or think about your idea? Then decide that you will look only to God's Word and the vision He has put in your heart to know what you can accomplish.

- If there is something important in your life that you have left unfinished, or something you've always wanted to do "someday," decide now to take steps to accomplish it. Write down the specific steps needed and begin to address them.

- As Dr. Munroe said, you cannot try to meet every need around you and still be effective in helping people. The purpose God has given you is meant to keep you centered on what is most important for you to be involved in. Have you been trying to "do everything"? If so, evaluate your commitments and activities. Then decide what you are meant to be involved in based on your purpose according to God's will and Word.

Praying about It

- Pray to God about your past failures and other circumstances that have seemed to hinder your vision. Remember that God is a restorer and that He will put back in you what life has taken out. Ask Him to renew His vision within you, and to help you lay aside the past and move forward in His purposes.

- As you continue to pray about your vision, set a destination for your life and trust that God will guide you where you need to go.

YOU ARE NOT DEFINED BY YOUR PAST OR CONFINED BY EXTERNAL FACTORS.

NOTES

Chapter Four
Principle #1:
Be Directed by a Clear Vision

To fulfill your vision, you must have a clear guiding purpose for your life.

CHAPTER THEME

Every effective leader or group of people in history has had one thing in common: They were directed by a clear vision. Having a guiding purpose for your life is perhaps the single most important key to fulfilling your dream. You personally, as an individual, must have your own guiding life vision. This vision must be absolutely clear to you because, otherwise, you will have nothing to aim at, and you will achieve nothing.

Question for Reflection

1. What is your personal vision? Try to write it in one sentence.

Exploring Principles and Purposes

2. What did Dr. Munroe say he discovered was the key to life? (pp. 82–83)

3. If you are lazy or bored, what does this show about you? (p. 83)

_____

_____

4. To have vision, you must _____ where you want to go in life and then be _____ and _____ in carrying it out. (p. 83)

5. What is the difference between having a true work and having just a job? (p. 85)

_____

_____

_____

6. Once your vision becomes clear to you, how will you feel until you are able to take action on it? (pp. 85–86)

_____

_____

7. What is one of the most significant questions you must answer for yourself? (p. 86)

_____

_____

8. What is the first thing you should do in answering this question? (p. 87)

_____

_____

9. In order to find your vision, what must you be in touch with? (p. 86)

_____

_____

10. Your vision should be something that _____ _____ after you're gone, something that has greater lasting power than _____. (pp. 86–87)

11. Give a definition of vision that expresses its forward-looking quality. (p. 87)

12. Vision demands _____ by its very nature. (p. 87)

13. Although vision is often associated with solving problems, why will vision be active in your life even when things are going well? (p. 88)

14. In living our lives, why shouldn't we try to go back to the "good old days"? (p. 88)

15. Vision is always _____-focused. We need to _____ _____ the past, but we cannot _____ to it. (p. 88)

16. Because vision involves change and new ways of thinking, it can keep you constantly unsettled. Yet how does this continual newness help you in the process of fulfilling your life's purpose? (p. 88)

17. A clear vision gives us a _____ that keeps us continually _____ _____ in life. (p. 89)

Conclusion

Whether you are young, middle-aged, or older, if you don't have a clear purpose, you are going to be distracted by the many demands and options of everyday life, because the world is an extremely busy place. Even when you do set your mind on what you want to do, all the other business of the world will try to get in the way of it. A clear guiding vision will enable you to have focus in life and to move forward toward a specific purpose when you are tempted to be distracted by lesser or nonessential things.

Applying the Principles of Vision

Thinking It Over

- Are you able to answer the question, "What is it that I want?" Why or why not? What would it take for you to be able to answer it?

- Think about your vision until you have a strong image of your preferable future, a clear conception of something which is not yet reality, but which can exist.

- Are you involved in your true work or just a job? Is something bothering you or making you depressed because you know you should be doing it but haven't done it yet? What do you need to do to get ready for your true work?

- Is your vision for your life something that will live on after you're gone, or is it merely a desire for the accumulation of possessions to enjoy today? What can you invest in that will outlast you?

Acting on It

- What things in your life are distracting you from the real "business" of your life? Make a plan to refocus on your vision.

- If you have a tendency to want to return to the "good old days," remember that you can build on the past but are meant to progress in what God has planned for you. First, think about how tradition and memories of good things are affecting your progress in your vision. Then, glean the good from the past, but make plans to move forward in your vision.

- Do you have a positive or negative attitude toward change in your life? Instead of focusing on the unsettling part of change, remind yourself that the constant newness and fluctuation of vision prepares you to recognize and take the next step toward your purpose. Learn to appreciate this role of change in your life.

Praying about It

- Ask God to confirm what He has put in your heart for you to do.

- Being in touch with the values and priorities of the kingdom of God will help you to find your vision. Make it a point to pray and read the Bible daily to better understand God's ways and to receive guidance and wisdom from Him.

YOUR VISION WILL BOTHER YOU UNTIL YOU TAKE ACTION ON IT.

NOTES

NOTES

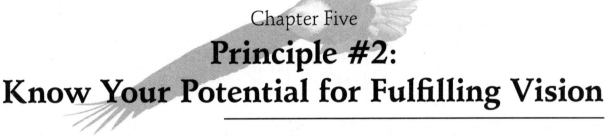

Chapter Five
Principle #2:
Know Your Potential for Fulfilling Vision

WHEN YOU DISCOVER YOUR DREAM, YOU WILL ALSO DISCOVER
YOUR ABILITY TO FULFILL IT.

CHAPTER THEME

In order to fulfill your vision, you must also come into an awareness of your potential. Potential is who you really are, in accordance with your vision. Potential is the person who has been trapped inside you because of false ideas (your own or others') of who you are. Potential is hidden capacity, untapped power, unreleased energy. It is all you could be but haven't yet become. God has created you to do something wonderful, and He has given you all of the abilities and resources you need to do it.

Question for Reflection

1. How much potential do you think you have for fulfilling your vision? Why?

_____

_____

_____

_____

Exploring Principles and Purposes

2. What determines your potential for fulfilling your vision? (p. 91)

_____

3. Whatever you were born to do, you are _____ to do. (p. 91)

4. God gives _____ to fulfill _____
_____. (p. 91)

43

5. What has God placed within you that is more than enough potential for the needs of your purpose? (p. 92)

6. What you are able to accomplish has to do with— [choose one] (p. 92)

   (a) who your parents were.

   (b) the power of God's Spirit working in you.

   (c) your physical attributes.

   (d) your past.

7. What will God do for you in terms of what you can ask for or imagine? (p. 92)

8. Once Dr. Munroe learned the truth of what God could do for him, what did it enable him to do? (p. 93)

9. Why did God give you the gift of imagination? (p. 93)

10. What should you be doing on a regular basis to help you achieve your vision? (p. 93)

11. Who shouldn't you allow to judge your potential? Why? (p. 94)

12. God designed and built you for the fulfillment of your vision. This means that you are _____ for your purpose. (p. 94)

13. Why did God give you dreams for your life? (p. 94)

14. Why does God appoint, anoint, and distinguish people? (p. 95)

15. When is the ability to accomplish your vision manifested? (p. 95)

16. What might your present job contain in terms of your vision? (p. 95)

17. What should you do with the "seed" of the vision God has placed within you? (p. 96)

Conclusion

God will never call you to an assignment without giving you the provision for accomplishing it. If you understand this principle, no one can stop you from fulfilling your vision. You were born with the potential for the fulfillment of your destiny, which has already been established within you. When you discover your dream, you will also discover your ability. You can always determine what you can do by the dream that is within you.

Applying the Principles of Vision

Thinking It Over

- Have you said yes to your dream and started to act on it? Why or why not?

- Has your perspective on your potential to fulfill your vision changed as a result of reading this chapter? Why or why not?

- Are there things about yourself or your life that you thought limited your potential for achieving your vision (e.g., a physical attribute, your ethnic background, your current resources)? If so, what perspective should you have on these perceived limitations?

- While people can give us valuable insight into our strengths and weaknesses, our gifts and abilities, sometimes they may not recognize our potential. Have you been allowing another person to judge your potential? What is the criteria for your potential in achieving your vision?

Acting on It

- Take a "virtual tour" of your dream. Imagine all the details of the completed vision. Then let God know that is where you want to go. Ask Him to enable you to take your idea from dream to full-fledged reality.

- Plant the seed of your vision today by beginning to act on it; then immediately nurture it by placing your faith in God and His purposes for you.

- Commit the following Scripture verse to memory: *"Now to him who is able to do immeasurably* ["exceeding abundantly" KJV] *more than all we ask or imagine, according to his power that is at work within us"* (Ephesians 3:20).

Praying about It

- Think about your vision and what it will require. Then write down what you are now able to do or will be able to do—as needs arise—through God's purpose and provision for you. Take each requirement or need and thank God that He will meet it at just the right time.

- Seek to obey God in all things and ask Him to work in your life through the power of His Spirit to enable you to fulfill your vision.

- Thank God for your present job and ask Him to use it to prepare you for your true life's work.

WHATEVER GOD CALLS FOR, HE PROVIDES FOR. WHATEVER HE REQUIRES, HE ENABLES YOU TO DO.

NOTES

Chapter Six
Principle #3:
Develop a Concrete Plan for Your Vision

To man belong the plans of the heart.
—Proverbs 16:1

CHAPTER THEME

People often think their dreams will just happen. They find out later, after they have sadly wasted many years of their lives, that this is not the case. Jesus said that a wise person doesn't start to build something unless he first works out the details. God Himself had a plan when He created humanity.

None of us can move toward our dreams without a plan. Ideas are seeds of destiny planted by God in the minds of humankind. Yet how does that destiny come to pass? When ideas are cultivated, they become imagination. Imagination, if it is watered and developed, becomes a plan. Finally, if a plan is followed, it becomes a reality.

Question for Reflection

1. Does planning currently play a role in your pursuit of short-term and long-term goals? Why or why not?

_____

_____

_____

_____

Exploring Principles and Purposes

2. There is no _____ without planning. (p. 99)

3. What did Dr. Munroe realize as a teenager about receiving God's guidance for his life? (p. 100)

4. What two verses from Proverbs indicate that God wants you to make a plan for the vision that is in your heart? (p. 100)

5. When you receive an idea from God, what must you soon do with the idea? (p. 100)

6. What will happen if you never take action on your idea? (p. 100)

7. When you lack a plan, what will you likely miss out on? (p. 101)

8. A contractor continually consults his blueprints to see if his building is being constructed correctly. Similarly, if you don't have a plan for your life, you will have nothing to refer to when you want to make sure you are _____ _____ with your vision. (p. 102)

9. Developing a blueprint for your vision begins with answering two vital questions. What is the first question? (p. 102)

10. You will never become really successful in your life if you don't have a clear idea of your own _____ in _____. (p. 102)

11. What is the second question you must answer?

12. Once you learn God's purpose, you can start planning effectively because you will be able to plan with _____. (p. 102)

13. When does a vision become a plan? (p. 102)

14. Your part is to write the plan. What is God's part? (p. 103)

15. What has God given you that will enable you to develop a plan for your vision? (p. 103)

16. Why can't you tell your plan to everyone when you are first developing it? (p. 104)

17. Why is your dream worth writing down? (p. 104)

18. When Nehemiah gave credit to God for his vision and how it was coming to pass, what was the result in the lives of those who were going to work on the project? (p. 105)

19. Your plan is material for your _____. (p. 105)

20. You were designed for destiny. Make a plan and _____ it. (p. 106)

Conclusion

The Bible says that God will give you the desires of your heart if you will delight in Him (Psalm 37:4). However, it also implies that God will direct your steps once you make a concrete plan to move toward what you desire. Have you expressed to God what is in your heart, and have you presented Him with your plan for accomplishing it? What are you waiting for?

Applying the Principles of Vision

Thinking It Over

• Have you been trying to fulfill your vision without a clear plan? What have you learned in this chapter about the significance of planning?

• Have you ever had an idea from God that you didn't act upon, and then saw someone else develop? If so, how did you feel when you saw that happen? What will you do with the ideas God gives you?

• Take some time to think about the following statement: If God gave you your vision, it deserves to be done.

Acting on It

• Do you have answers to the questions "Who am I?" and "Where am I going?" Start the process of developing a blueprint for your vision by writing down answers to these questions. To help you do this, answer the questions on pages 218–19 of chapter seventeen and write out a mission statement for your life based on the guidelines on page 225 of *The Principles and Power of Vision*. Remember that it is knowing your true identity that will give you the ability and courage to write your life plan.

• Start thinking about where you want to be one, five, ten, twenty, thirty, even fifty years from now. Jot down your ideas and continue to refine and pray about them.

- Keep Proverbs 16 verses 1 and 9 in front of you as you begin to develop your plan in order to remind yourself of two key truths: The Lord will work out the details of how and when the plan will be accomplished, and He will direct you in carrying out your vision.

"To man belong the plans of the heart, but from the LORD comes the reply of the tongue."
(Proverbs 16:1)

"In his heart a man plans his course, but the LORD determines his steps." (Proverbs 16:9)

Praying about It

- If you are still unsure of your answers to the questions "Who am I?" and "Where am I going?" ask God to continue to reveal them to you as you worship Him, pray, read His Word, and come to understand the vision He has put in your heart.

- Express to God the vision that is in your heart, and present Him with your overall plan for accomplishing it, even if your plan is in the early stages. As you develop and refine your plan in the weeks, months, and years ahead, keep offering it to God and trust Him to work out all the details of how the vision will be accomplished.

- Since your plan is material for your prayers, take specific aspects of your plan and ask for God's wisdom, guidance, and strength in carrying them out.

YOUR PLAN WILL ENABLE YOU TO FULFILL YOUR DESTINY.

NOTES

NOTES

Chapter Seven
Principle #4:
Possess the Passion of Vision

FOR THE PEOPLE WORKED WITH ALL THEIR HEART.
—NEHEMIAH 4:6

CHAPTER THEME

You'll never be successful in fulfilling your personal vision if you do not have a passion for it. Are you hungry for your vision? How badly do you want what you're going after? Passion is stamina that says, "I'm going to go after this, no matter what happens. If I have to wait ten years, I'm going to get it." If you want to go all the way to your dream, you can't sit back and expect everything to be easy. You must have a purpose that produces passion.

Question for Reflection

1. On a scale of 1–10, ten being greatest, how would you rate your current desire to fulfill your vision?

1   2   3   4   5   6   7   8   9   10

Exploring Principles and Purposes

2. What have passionate people discovered? (p. 109)

3. Giving up _____ _____ and _____ for your genuine vision is the path to true life. (p. 109)

4. What is one reason Dr. Munroe kept stressing the need for a clear guiding purpose in life? (p. 110)

5. Why did Paul give a list of problems and tribulations as part of the proof that he was a genuine apostle? (pp. 111–13)

6. _____ to vision is one of the marks of its legitimacy. (p. 111)

7. If you're going to go after your vision, what can you expect to experience? (p. 113)

8. Persistence will keep you moving forward, yet you need _____ to _____ your persistence. (p. 113)

9. If you can stop working on your vision and still be happy, or if you can be so discouraged by setbacks that you give up on your dream, what does this show about you? (p. 113)

10. Why do many people fail to win at pursuing their visions? (p. 114)

11. No matter how tough things are, what perspective does a passionate person have? (p. 114)

12. A person of passion is always _____ to fulfill his vision. (p. 114)

13. What is passion willing to do? (p. 115)

14. Passion helps you to stay _____ on your vision. (p. 115)

15. If you become passionate about your vision, you can _____ _____ _____ and persevere to the _____ of your goals. (p. 116)

Conclusion

Whenever you are tempted to quit too soon or to stay down when life knocks you over, remember the examples of Nehemiah and Paul. Passion is an urge that is deeper than any resistance it might encounter. It is a goal to win that is bigger than the desire to quit. Capture your vision and stay with it, and you will be rewarded with seeing that vision become a reality, no matter who or what might try to come against it.

Applying the Principles of Vision

Thinking It Over

- If your rating for question 1 was in the middle range or lower, what have you read in this chapter that can help you increase your passion for your vision?

- It is genuine vision that produces real passion. If you lack passion, might you still be trying to follow a false or self-serving purpose in life?

- Do you generally give up the first time you fall down, and do you stop at the least resistance? In what ways might you have become discouraged or complacent about your vision? What will you do to regain your passion for your dream and remain faithful to it?

Acting on It

- Write down specific problems and tribulations that have tested/are testing your vision. Then write down how you will respond to them based on what you've learned in this chapter.

- Since vision is the precedent for passion, remind yourself of your vision each day. Go on continual tours of your dream. Imagine it until it is so clear and present in your mind that it produces a passion that makes you move forward and persevere to its fulfillment.

- Meditate on the following Scripture passages to help yourself focus on the importance of passion in fulfilling your purpose:

Whatever you do, work at it with all your heart, as working for the Lord, not for men, since you know that you will receive an inheritance from the Lord as a reward.

(Colossians 3:23–24)

I press on to take hold of that for which Christ Jesus took hold of me....One thing I do: Forgetting what is behind and straining toward what is ahead, I press on toward the goal to win the prize for which God has called me heavenward in Christ Jesus.

(Philippians 3:12–14)

Praying about It

- Each morning, thank God that He has given you another day that you can use to take the next step to the fulfillment of your vision. Ask Him to lead and guide you during the day toward His purpose for you.

- Ask God to help you to remain faithful to the vision He has given you, no matter what the circumstances.

YOU MUST HAVE PURPOSE THAT PRODUCES PASSION.

NOTES

Chapter Eight
Principle #5:
Develop the Faith of Vision

SIGHT IS A FUNCTION OF THE EYES, WHILE VISION IS A
FUNCTION OF THE HEART.

CHAPTER THEME

Most people have physical sight but no vision. Physical sight is the ability to see things as they are. Vision is the capacity to see things as they could or should be, and that takes faith. You must develop the faith of vision if you are to fulfill your dream.

Question for Reflection

1. What do you think Helen Keller meant by her statement, "What's worse than being blind is having sight without vision"?

Exploring Principles and Purposes

2. What is sight a function of? What is vision a function of? (p. 119)

3. You must never let what your eyes see determine what your heart _____. (p. 120)

4. What are you to walk according to? (p. 120)

5. When you have vision, you are governed by the _____ God has put in your heart. (p. 120)

6. According to Hebrews 11:1, what is faith? (p. 120)

7. How did Dr. Munroe define faith, based on the answers to the previous two questions? (p. 120)

8. Why is sight without vision dangerous? (pp. 120–21)

9. The vision in your heart is greater than your _____. (p. 121)

10. How were you designed to operate in life? (p. 121)

11. How does God function in faith? (p. 122)

12. While thoughts are the most _____ things on earth, words are the most _____. (p. 123)

13. When you speak words expressing what you see in your vision, what happens? (p. 123)

14. What is one way you can undermine your vision? (p. 123)

15. What does faith see problems as? (pp. 124–25)

16. To do great things, you first need to— [choose one] (p. 125)

    (a) be lucky.
    (b) think and expect great things.
    (c) be great.
    (d) all of the above

17. _____ control the world. (p. 125)

18. Complete the following: A vision is an idea that is so powerful _____
    _____. (p. 125)

19. Why is the faith of vision crucial? (p. 126)

Conclusion

The greatest gift that God gave humankind is not the gift of sight, but the gift of vision. Faith is vision in the heart. Proverbs 23:7 says, "As [a person] *thinks in his heart, so is he*" (NKJV). The success or failure of your dream will be determined by how you see. Do you have sight or vision?

Applying the Principles of Vision

Thinking It Over

• What is your answer to the question that concluded this chapter: Do you have sight or vision? Why?

- Are you thinking and speaking in positive or negative terms in relation to your vision? How might what you are thinking and speaking be undermining your vision?

- Do you see life's difficulties as problems or opportunities? Why? What can you do to focus more on the opportunities than the problems?

- In what way(s) can your vision outlive you?

Acting on It

- Great thinking precedes great achievement. Write down great thoughts about your dream and repeat them aloud to yourself daily. As Dr. Munroe wrote earlier, don't sell yourself short in choosing your life's vision.

- You can help protect your vision by guarding what you say. If you have been speaking negatively about your vision, choose one aspect of it and begin to speak words of faith regarding it.

- Worry and fear will make your vision short-circuit. Memorize Scriptures to help build your faith, such as the following:

And we know that in all things God works for the good of those who love him, who have been called according to his purpose. (Romans 8:28)

My God will meet all [my] *needs according to his glorious riches in Christ Jesus.* (Philippians 4:19)

The one who calls you is faithful and he will do it. (1 Thessalonians 5:24)

- For your vision to outlive you, you must clearly conceive and express your ideas. Continue to define and refine your vision until it is very clear to you. Express your vision not only to yourself but to others who are close to you and support your vision.

Praying about It

- Ask God to help you clarify your vision and to fill you with great thoughts about it so you can speak specific words of faith concerning it.

- Read the following Scripture passages and pray that God will give you greater insight about faith through them: Mark 4:35–41; Matthew 21:19–22; Mark 6:34–44; John 11:1–44. Then put your faith into practice in regard to your vision.

FAITH IS SEEING THE FUTURE IN THE PRESENT.

Notes

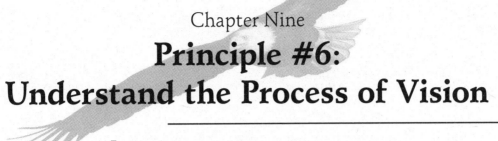

Chapter Nine

Principle #6:
Understand the Process of Vision

IN HIS HEART A MAN PLANS HIS COURSE,
BUT THE LORD DETERMINES HIS STEPS.
—PROVERBS 16:9

CHAPTER THEME

There is no hurried way to get to God's vision. Proverbs 16:9 says, *"In his heart a man plans his course, but the LORD determines his steps."* Notice the word *"steps."* God didn't say He would direct our leaps, but rather our steps. He leads us step-by-step, day-by-day, through tribulations, trials, and character-building opportunities as He moves us toward our dreams. Why does God lead us in this way? Because He doesn't want us only to win; He wants us to win with style. God's desire is to fashion people with character and battle scars who can say, "God didn't just hand me this vision. I have qualified for it."

Questions for Reflection

1. How long do you expect it will take you to fulfill your vision?

2. Do you feel anxious that your vision isn't being fulfilled as quickly as you would like? Why or why not?

Exploring Principles and Purposes

3. God has a plan for each of our lives. How does He usually bring those plans to pass? (p. 129)

4. While God tells you where you are going with your vision, what will He rarely tell you? (p. 129)

5. At the time you receive your vision, you are not yet _____ for it. (p. 130)

6. The process God is taking you through to arrive at your destination is designed to do what? (p. 130)

7. What are two things that the process of vision will do for you? (p. 130)

8. What might happen if God showed you exactly what is going to happen in your life as you progress toward your vision? (pp. 130–33)

9. Though God's ways of getting you where you need to go will often be different from what you expect, there will always be a _____ _____ for them. (p. 132)

10. Your hardships are part of God's _____ _____ for you. (p. 132)

11. When we go through difficult times, what do we often think is happening? What is really the case? (p. 132)

12. What is God trying to do in our lives when we're grumbling that He is taking too long to fulfill our visions? (p. 133)

13. Sometimes, we want the vision without being _____ for it. (p. 133)

14. When will your vision culminate? (p. 134)

15. If you're in a job that is not your true occupation, what should you be doing while you have the job? (p. 134)

16. What does purpose give to your present job? (p. 134)

17. As you wait for your dream, how must you live? (p. 135)

Conclusion

At the time when you receive your vision, you don't yet have the ability to handle the big things that you're dreaming. You don't have the experience or the character for them. The vision that you have received awaits an appointed time. You must believe in what God has told you about your vision because it won't happen overnight. It will occur through a process of character development, which will come about as you live by faith and inner vision—not by what you see right now.

Applying the Principles of Vision

Thinking It Over

- Is the process of fulfilling your vision different from what you expected? Why or why not? If so, has this unexpected route caused you to become discouraged or even to abandon the vision? Are you thinking, "Where is the God of my vision?" Do you think He has stopped working to fulfill your purpose? If so, how will you respond to these feelings based on what you have read in this chapter?

- Right now, do you have enough discipline and character to fulfill your vision and still be faithful to God, your family, and other people? Why or why not?

- Are you submitting to the process of your vision or resisting it? What can you do to accept the process so you can move forward in God's purposes for you?

- Do you trust that your hardships are part of God's perfect plan for you? What have you learned about the value of hardships in the process of fulfilling your vision?

- Would you want your vision without being qualified for it? Why or why not?

Acting on It

- In this chapter, we've looked at the processes that Joseph, Moses, Daniel, Paul, and Jesus Christ went through to fulfill their visions. Start writing the story of your journey toward your own vision, even though you don't yet know how it will all come to pass. As you write, try to answer these questions: How has God used circumstances in my life to build character in me? What character qualities has God shown me that I still need to work on? What experience, knowledge, and skills am I gaining through my job and other avenues in my life? How have I seen God help me in the midst of my struggles? In what ways have I overcome temptation in my life? Write down the lessons you are learning and what God is teaching you. Keep an ongoing record of the process of your vision so you can see the hand of God in your life.

- Read Habakkuk 2:1–4. Then review the seven principles of vision based on this Scripture passage that are found on pages 227–28 of *The Principles and Power of Vision* to remind yourself that your vision will come to pass in God's timing.

- When you are tempted to think that God has abandoned you and your vision, read the following Scripture verses:

Surely I am with you always, to the very end of the age.   (Matthew 28:20)

Never will I leave you; never will I forsake you.   (Hebrews 13:5)

Can a mother forget the baby at her breast and have no compassion on the child she has borne? Though she may forget, I will not forget you! See, I have engraved you on the palms of my hands.   (Isaiah 49:15–16)

Praying about It

- As you progress toward your vision, have you been praying, "Lord, isn't there any other way?" God knows what you're going through because His Son felt the same way in the Garden of Gethsemane. Jesus is now interceding on your behalf (see Hebrews 7:25), and you can count on His strength and help. Therefore, just as Jesus did, change your prayer to, *"Yet not as I will, but as you will"* (Matthew 26:39), and trust God to bring you through to victory.

- Instead of complaining about how things are going in your life, exercise your faith in God and fill your heart with praise and worship to Him.

GOD PREPARES YOU FOR THE PURPOSE THROUGH THE PROCESS.

NOTES

NOTES

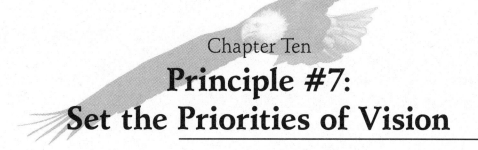

Chapter Ten

Principle #7:
Set the Priorities of Vision

YOUR LIFE IS THE SUM TOTAL OF THE DECISIONS YOU MAKE EVERY DAY.

CHAPTER THEME

If you want to be successful, you must set priorities for yourself in relation to your vision. Both successful and unsuccessful people alike make decisions every day that influence their chances of achieving their visions. Whether they realize it or not, it is the nature and quality of the choices they make that determine their success or failure.

Question for Reflection

1. Think of the most significant decision you have made in the last three years. Was this decision beneficial or harmful to your life and vision? Why?

Exploring Principles and Purposes

2. Why will understanding priority help you to accomplish your dream? (p. 137)

3. What do your choices and preferences reveal about you? (p. 137)

4. What did Dr. Munroe say has significantly contributed to who you are today? (p. 137)

5. How can you tell (for the most part) what kind of life you're going to have in the future? (pp. 137–38)

6. Because they determine your destiny, _____ and _____ are the most powerful words you will ever say. (p. 138)

7. When people don't succeed in their visions, it is often because they don't understand an important truth about prioritizing. What is that truth? (p. 138)

8. Circle one: True or False

    Even if something is a good thing, it is not necessarily beneficial to you. (p. 139)

9. How do you determine what is beneficial to you? (pp. 138–39)

10. Your greatest challenge is not in choosing between good or bad but between good and _____. (p. 140)

11. Why might you keep drifting off in the wrong direction in terms of your vision? (p. 141)

12. For what reason might you end up in a place where you don't really want to be in life? (pp. 142–43)

13. How can you make sure you will hit the mark? (p. 143)

14. Why do people sometimes become involved in too many things? (p. 143)

15. You will never be _____ in your life until you have real vision. (p. 145)

16. If you are afraid to take decisive action to move toward your vision, what should your perspective be? (p. 147)

17. What do people who succeed do? What happens when people don't do this? (p. 147)

Conclusion

Vision is the key to an effective life because when you see your destination, it helps you to discipline your life in ways that train, prepare, and provide for your vision. You must come to the point where you focus on what is necessary to fulfill your dream. If you don't, you won't make it to the end of your vision. If you have gotten off track in life, it doesn't matter how young or old you are: Refocus on your vision and make strong and specific decisions that will lead you there.

Applying the Principles of Vision

Thinking It Over

- What have your life choices revealed about who you are and what you value?

- Will your current habits, actions, and choices affect your life positively or negatively in the future? Why?

- What in your life is good but not necessarily beneficial to you?

- What might you be doing for the purpose of making people think you are busy and capable rather than for the purpose of furthering your vision?

Acting on It

- Write out your answers to the discipline questions found on pages 145–46 of *The Principles and Power of Vision*. Add any other categories that apply. Then do the next exercise, below.

- Ask yourself, "What benefits me? What will move me toward my goal?" Write out priorities in each area of your life in relation to your vision.

- Determine what you need to eliminate or scale back on in your life in order to focus on your dream.

Praying about It

- To make sure you hit your mark, tell God sincerely that you want to join with His plan for your life. Then let His yoke guide you by reading His Word, staying in step with His ways, and following His guidance in your life.

- If you've gotten off track from your vision, confess to God honestly that you haven't made the best use of your time, gifts, and resources in the past, but that you're going to make the rest of your life count. Ask Him to help you to stick to the priorities you have set and to recommit to your priorities whenever you start to stray from your vision.

CHOOSE TO LIVE WELL.

NOTES

Chapter Eleven
Principle #8:
Recognize People's Influence on Vision

WHEN YOU BEGIN TO ACT ON YOUR VISION, IT WILL STIR UP BOTH THOSE WHO WANT TO HELP YOU AND THOSE WHO WANT TO HINDER YOU.

CHAPTER THEME

You must recognize people's influence on your vision. God has people who are prepared to work with you and encourage you, and they will be a blessing to you. The principle of influence has a twofold application, however, because people can have a negative impact on us as well as a positive one. Whether you realize it or not, the influence of those you spend time with has a powerful effect on how you will end up in life and on whether you will succeed or fail in your vision.

Question for Reflection

1. What person has been the most positive influence on your life/vision so far? In what way?

Exploring Principles and Purposes

2. Why do you need other people if you are going to be successful in your vision? (p. 151)

3. There will always be a need for _____ people in your life. (p. 152)

4. If you have no dream or do not begin to act on your dream, what will happen to the people who are supposed to help you with your vision? (p. 152)

5. When you begin to act on your vision, what will it stir up? (p. 152)

6. What is the law of association? (p. 152)

7. There are two words that most accurately describe influence: _____ and _____. (p. 152)

8. What do people have the potential to create? (p. 153)

9. Your environment determines your _____-_____, and your mind-set determines your _____. (p. 153)

10. In general, what kind of friends should you choose? (p. 153)

11. What three questions of influence should you be asking yourself truthfully and regularly as you progress toward your vision? (pp. 153–54)

12. Why may certain people become angry with you or even begin to hate you when you step out and do something that they have never done? (pp. 155, 157)

13. Who can sometimes be the most detrimental to the fulfillment of your vision? Why is this the case? (p. 155)

14. People who change the world have declared independence from _____ _____ _____. (p. 156)

15. When people oppose you and your vision, what should you do? (pp. 156–57)

16. In regard to the problems that come with the law of association, what three things should you do to protect your vision? (pp. 157–162)

17. Whom should you disassociate yourself from? (p. 158)

18. Why are there some people you should just be acquainted with (have limited association with)? (p. 160)

19. How can you protect your mental environment? (p. 161)

20. What type of people should you expand your association with? (p. 161)

Conclusion

We all need other people to guide, help, and encourage us along the path to fulfilling our visions. Because we need the influence of others, however, we are also in danger of the negative effects people may have on us if we—or they—are not careful. Therefore, it is crucial for us to guard our hearts, thoughts, attitudes, and ideas from being sabotaged by those around us. We must increase the positive influences in our lives and decrease the negative ones as we pursue our individual goals in tandem with others.

Applying the Principles of Vision

Thinking It Over

- Do you tend to think that you don't need other people to help you in your life/vision? After reading this chapter, what have you learned about the necessity of other people encouraging you and helping you to fulfill your life's vision?

- In what ways have you become like those with whom you spend time?

- Are your close friends and/or potential spouse going in the same direction you are, and are they supportive of your life goals? If not, are you willing to forfeit your true purpose and vision because of their influence?

- Are you sacrificing your dream because you are afraid of others' disapproval or opposition? What have you learned in this chapter about how to respond to this situation?

Acting on It

- Answer the three questions posed in the chapter:

  1. "With whom am I spending time?" Who are your closest friends? Who are the people you are confiding in?

2. "What are these people doing to me?" In other words, what do they have you listening to, reading, thinking, doing? Where do they have you going? What do they have you saying? How do they have you feeling? What do they have you settling for?

3. "Is what these people are doing to me a good thing in light of my vision?"

- Consider carefully whom you should disassociate from, have limited association with, and expand your association with. Above all, ask yourself: "Who can help me toward my goal? What person can I get close to and learn from?"

- Decide ahead of time how you will respond the next time someone is negative about your vision.

- Begin to act on your dream so that the people who are supposed to help you in your vision will be able to do so.

- Read chapter 16, "The Generational Nature of Vision," in *The Principles and Power of Vision*. Then think about what kind of influence *you* are being on your family, friends, and others. What kind of legacy are you building for the next generation? What kind of nutrients are you leaving in the soil of life?

Praying about It

- Ask God to give you discernment about the positive and negative effects people are having on you so that you can make wise decisions about the associations in your life.

- Seek God about whom you should spend more time with to help you mature and prepare to work in your vision.

- Thank God for those who are a positive influence in your life, and ask Him to enable you to be a blessing to them as well.

PROTECT YOUR MENTAL ENVIRONMENT.

NOTES

NOTES

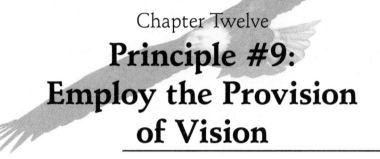

Chapter Twelve

Principle #9: Employ the Provision of Vision

GOD DESIGNED EVERY PURPOSE WITH ITS OWN PROSPERITY.

CHAPTER THEME

Many people stop dreaming about what they really want to do in life because they know they have few resources with which to do it. They believe they have to pay for their visions with their present incomes when sometimes they can barely make ends meet as it is. We must understand the power of provision if we are to fulfill our visions. God will never give you a vision without provision. The ability and resources are available for whatever you were born to do.

Question for Reflection

1. Does your vision sometimes seem unreachable because of all the resources it will take to accomplish it? What are your major concerns in achieving your vision? What is it about these concerns that seems most difficult to you?

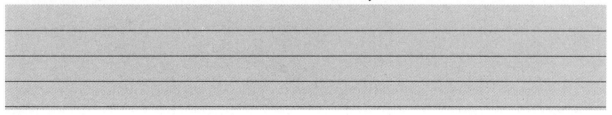

Exploring Principles and Purposes

2. Circle one: True or False

Our provisions are never equal to our visions at the moment we receive our visions. (p. 165)

3. To review, what is your job in regard to your vision? What is God's job? (p. 166)

4. What does this arrangement free you to be? (p. 166)

5. Why does God often give us dreams that confound us at first? (p. 166)

6. When does God manifest the provision for your vision? (pp. 166–67)

7. Whatever you were born to do _____ what you need to do it. (pp. 166–67)

8. What has God already blessed you with? (p. 167)

9. Dr. Munroe mentioned two misconceptions of prosperity. What are these misconceptions? (pp. 167–68)

10. Prosperity doesn't mean that tomorrow's need is met today; it means that _____ need is met today. (p. 169)

11. What does it mean to have true prosperity? (p. 170)

12. God has designed every purpose with its own _____. Your purpose
     has _____-_____ provision for it. (p. 171)

13. What is the nature and degree of your prosperity determined by? (p. 171)

14. Why will God sometimes not give us all the resources we need to fulfill our visions?
     (p. 172)

15. Why is obedience to your vision not just a private issue? (p. 173)

16. If God is not short of anything we need, why are there some things we might ask for
     that He can't supply us with? (p. 175)

17. There are five specific ways in which God provides resources to fulfill our visions.
     What is the first way? (pp. 176–79)

18. What efforts will you likely need to make in order to employ this provision? (pp. 178–79)

19. Name the second way God provides for our visions. (p. 179)

20. How did Dr. Munroe define work? (p. 179)

21. Work reveals your _____. (p. 180)

22. What is the third way God provides for our visions? (p. 182)

23. What is a large part of the gift of cultivation? (p. 182)

24. The fourth way God provides for our visions is by giving us wisdom to _____ and _____ for the future. (p. 183)

25. What is the fifth way God provides for vision? (p. 184)

Conclusion

Proverbs 16:1 says, *"To man belong the plans of the heart, but from the LORD comes the reply of the tongue."* Trust God to provide for your vision each step of the way, and let

Him reveal how you will obtain the finances, people, buildings, and anything else that is required. Always remember that purpose is your responsibility; provision is God's responsibility.

Applying the Principles of Vision

Thinking It Over

- Has your definition of prosperity changed as a result of reading this chapter? Why or why not?

- Have you been waiting for all the provision to be in place before starting to work on your vision? What have you learned in this chapter about that approach? What should your perspective on provision be?

- Dr. Munroe said that God provides for the birds, but He doesn't hand-deliver food to their nests. In what ways might you have been waiting for God to hand-deliver your provision instead of taking advantage of what God has supplied for your use?

- How much of your heavenly storehouse have you asked for?

- What is your vision of inheritance for your descendants?

Acting on It

- Make a point to get rid of any excess in your life that is detracting from your vision.

- What resources do you need to fulfill your dream? List them, and then trust God to provide for all the needs of your vision as He has promised to do.

- How will you use the information in this chapter to pursue provision for your vision?

- Meditate on and memorize the following Scripture passage to keep yourself from worrying about your material needs as you pursue your vision:

Therefore I tell you, do not worry about your life, what you will eat or drink; or about your body, what you will wear. Is not life more important than food, and the body more important than clothes?...So do not worry, saying, "What shall we eat?" or "What shall we drink?" or "What shall we wear?" For the pagans run after all these things, and your heavenly Father knows that you need them. But seek first his kingdom and his righteousness, and all these things will be given to you as well. (Matthew 6:25, 31–33)

Praying about It

- Ask God to forgive you if you have been worrying about your provision rather than trusting Him for it. Then thank Him that He will provide for all your needs as you seek and obey Him. Honor and worship Him as the God who provides for you.

• Use what is in your heavenly warehouse by daily praying with confidence, "Lord, please deliver to me what I need today according to the abundant provision You have stored up for me."

WHATEVER GOD PURPOSES, HE PROVIDES FOR.

NOTES

Chapter Thirteen

Principle #10:
Use Persistence in Achieving the Vision

EVERY TRUE VISION WILL BE TESTED FOR AUTHENTICITY.

CHAPTER THEME

It is inevitable that obstacles are going to come against you and your vision. You must not think that you are exempt from this reality or you won't understand how to achieve your vision. When you begin to act on your dream, everything is going to try to get in the way of it. You must be prepared for the challenges, for they are coming. God assures us that, even though there will be times of stress, disappointment, and pressure, the vision will come to pass. Therefore, it is not a matter of whether your vision is going to be fulfilled. Rather, it's a matter of whether you're going to be true to your vision in the midst of trials so that God can bring it to pass.

Question for Reflection

1. What are your thoughts on the following quotation from Eleanor Roosevelt: "A [person] is like a tea bag. You never know how strong it is until it's in hot water"? Have you found this to be true in your own life? In what ways?

Exploring Principles and Purposes

2. What does it mean to have faithfulness in regard to your vision? (p. 190)

3. What does it mean to be steadfast? (p. 190)

4. What should opposition do for you? (pp. 190–91)

5. Courage is the ability to _____ _____ in the face of _____. (p. 190)

6. Dr. Munroe mentioned three challenges or pressures we may experience in life. What is the first one? (p. 191)

7. What will help you overcome a difficult background and fulfill your purpose as God's child? (p. 191)

8. Name the second challenge or pressure we may experience in life. (pp. 191–92)

9. How should you respond to this second challenge? (p. 192)

10. What is the third challenge or pressure we may experience in life? (p. 192)

11. How can you overcome such opposition? (p. 192)

12. Destiny demands _____. (p. 193)

13. When it comes to their visions, persistent people win because they never do what? (p. 194)

14. According to Dr. Munroe, how strong is the light of God's vision in your heart? (p. 196)

15. What does *perseverance* mean? (p. 196)

16. _____ is formed by pressure. (p. 197)

17. How does God use pressure in your life? (p. 197)

18. What will happen when you understand that pressure is good for you? (p. 197)

19. The Scriptures say that people who succeed are those who— [choose one] (p. 197)

    (a) endure to the end.

    (b) outrun others.

    (c) step on others.

    (d) are smarter than others.

20. Every true vision will be tested for _____. (p. 198)

21. What benefits can you gain from a crisis? (p. 198)

Conclusion

Don't be afraid when you make a declaration of what you're going to do in life and difficulty follows—it comes to test your resolve. If your vision is authentic, life is going to try it, just to make sure. Therefore, if you are encountering opposition to your vision, be encouraged that your faith is being strengthened and that God is not only enabling you to stand strong in the face of difficulties, but also to overcome them so you can fulfill His purpose for you.

Applying the Principles of Vision

Thinking It Over

- What do you usually do when you are put in "hot water"? Do you allow yourself to be burned, or do you make tea?

- Have you accepted the cost of your vision? In what areas of your life/vision are you in need of perseverance?

- What will you do the next time Life says no to your vision?

Acting on It

- List the major challenges and pressures you are encountering in regard to your vision. What constructive actions can you take in response to these challenges and pressures? How can you persevere under them and use them for your benefit (e.g., to make you stronger and wiser)?

- When you are feeling overwhelmed with the obstacles that you are facing, read this Scripture passage and remind yourself that God loves you, has given you your vision, and will enable you to be victorious:

Who shall separate us from the love of Christ? Shall trouble or hardship or persecution or famine or nakedness or danger or sword?...No, in all these things we are more than conquerors through Him who loved us [and called us and gave us our visions].

(Romans 8:35, 37)

- Write down the saying "Destiny demands diligence" on a piece of paper and put it where you can be reminded of it every day.

Praying about It

- Pray that God will give you a willing spirit so that you will yield to His work in you and allow Him to form your character through the pressures of life. Ask Him specifically to develop faithfulness, steadfastness, and courage in you.

- When you feel beaten up by life, go to God in prayer and ask Him to cool you with the water of His Word, bring healing to your wounds through the ointment of the Holy Spirit, and fill you with renewed vision. After you are strengthened, be sure to move forward in your vision with persistence.

**THE VISION IN YOUR HEART MUST BE GREATER
THAN ANY OPPOSITION TO IT.**

NOTES

NOTES

Chapter Fourteen

Principle #11:
Be Patient in the Fulfillment of Vision

IMITATE THOSE WHO THROUGH FAITH AND PATIENCE INHERIT
WHAT HAS BEEN PROMISED.
—HEBREWS 6:12

CHAPTER THEME

It may take a while for your vision to come to fruition, but if you are willing to wait for it (which many people are not), it will come to pass. People who have long patience will always win.

Questions for Reflection

1. Who is the most patient person you know? Why?

2. What qualities does a patient person have?

Exploring Principles and Purposes

3. According to Hebrews 10:35–36, what will be the result of your having patience or persevering? What else does it say you must do to receive this result? (p. 203)

4. Patience _____ the eventual success of the plan. (p. 203)

5. What do some people do when making plans to carry out their visions that is counter-productive? (p. 203)

6. Why do you need to patiently rely on God's guidance every step of the way? (p. 204)

7. At what time will your vision come to pass? (p. 204)

8. With what attitude should you wait for your vision? [choose one] (p. 204)

   (a) boredom
   (b) discouragement
   (c) anxiety
   (d) anticipation

9. You must be willing to progress at the vision's _____. (p. 204)

10. When you are patient in the fulfillment of your vision, what are you able to be in the midst of uncertainty? (p. 205)

11. How can you endure the "cross" of life's difficulties while waiting for your vision? (p. 205)

12. Vision takes _____ and patience and often involves _____. (p. 205)

13. Patience is the key to power over what things? (p. 205)

14. In what way is patience more powerful than might in a person? (p. 206)

15. In the last chapter, we learned that trials test our faith. According to James 1:3 (NKJV), what does this testing of our faith produce? (p. 206)

16. According to James 1:4 (NKJV), what does patience then do for us? (p. 206)

Conclusion

It's crucial that you maintain your dream by patiently waiting for its fulfillment. Jesus came to earth in the fullness of time, and so will your vision. If someone asks you about your vision, you can say, "I'm just waiting for the next move." Some people might wonder if it will ever happen. You do not need to wonder, however, but simply to wait with confidence and anticipation. Remember that God takes you through a step-by-step process as He makes you ready to enjoy, work in, and be a blessing through your vision.

Applying the Principles of Vision

Thinking It Over

- Have you been trying to force the timetable of the fulfillment of your vision? If so, what have you learned about patience in this chapter that will enable you to trust God to fulfill the vision in His timing?

- With what attitude have you been waiting for your vision? On what basis can you wait with eagerness, peace, and anticipation?

- Based on what you have learned about the power of patience in Proverbs 16:32, how can patience enable you to overcome opposition in your life? *"Better a patient man than a warrior, a man who controls his temper than one who takes a city."*

Acting on It

- Develop patience as you wait for your vision by focusing on the joy that is set before you—the fulfillment of your dream—so that you will endure to see it come to pass. (See Hebrews 12:2.)

- Have you allowed the testing of your faith to produce patience in you? Keep a record of how your faith is tested, and ask God to help you develop the all-important quality of patience through these various trials so that you can live in the purposes He has for you.

- Strengthen your spirit as you patiently wait for your vision to come to pass by committing these verses to memory:

But let patience have its perfect work, that you may be perfect and complete, lacking nothing. (James 1:4 NKJV)

We do not want you to become lazy, but to imitate those who through faith and patience inherit what has been promised. (Hebrews 6:12)

You need to persevere ["have need of patience" KJV] so that when you have done the will of God, you will receive what he has promised. (Hebrews 10:36)

Praying about It

- Acknowledge to God that you are relying on His guidance every step of the way because He alone knows all that is needed, both within you and outside you, to bring your vision to pass.

- As you wait for your vision, use the time to draw close to God and learn to follow the subtle leading of His Holy Spirit in your life so that you know when He is saying, *"This is the way; walk in it"* (Isaiah 30:21).

"LET US RUN WITH PATIENCE THE RACE THAT IS SET BEFORE US."
—HEBREWS 12:1 KJV

NOTES

Chapter Fifteen
Principle #12:
Stay Connected to the Source of Vision

I AM THE VINE; YOU ARE THE BRANCHES....
APART FROM ME YOU CAN DO NOTHING.
—JOHN 15:5

CHAPTER THEME

If you are going to be successful in your vision, you must have a daily, dynamic personal prayer life with God. You need continual communion and fellowship with the Source of vision.

Question for Reflection

1. Have you noticed a difference in your life between the times when you were praying and reading the Bible regularly and the times when you were not? If so, what were those differences?

Exploring Principles and Purposes

2. God is not only the _____ of your vision, but also your continuing _____ as you progress toward its fulfillment. (p. 209)

3. Apart from God, how much of His purpose are you able to accomplish? [See John 15:5.] (p. 209)

4. What will happen if you stay in touch with God? (p. 209)

5. Prayer sustains you in the _____ of vision. (p. 209)

6. Through what kind of prayer will God bring you through your difficulties and give you the victory? (p. 210)

7. What will God do for you when you get away from the noise and confusion of life and go to Him with your discouragement and stress? (p. 210)

8. Through our prayers, God encourages us to get back out into the _____ of faith. (p. 210)

9. Since prayer is where you receive the ability to continue the fight, what is it crucial for you to find during the day? (p. 211)

10. Prayer is the essential _____ of vision. (p. 211)

11. When people attack your dream, what should you do? (p. 212)

12. What *shouldn't* you do? (p. 212)

13. Because God is the One who planted your life's purpose within you in the beginning and has invested Himself in your dream, what can you be assured of? (p. 212)

Conclusion

You will never achieve your vision without prayer because prayer is what keeps you connected to the Vision-Giver. Visions can be very demanding. Sometimes, in the pursuit of your vision, you will grow emotionally and spiritually weary if things don't seem to be working out for you. When you have been pressed, criticized, and opposed, you can become weak in faith and not want to go on. Yet Philippians 1:6 says, *"He who began a good work in you will carry it on to completion."* Therefore, continually go to God in prayer and allow Him to give you new strength and hope to persevere to the completion of your vision. There may be times when the only resource you have is prayer. Yet that is all you will need. God will see you through.

Applying the Principles of Vision

Thinking It Over

- When people attack you, do you try to answer or retaliate against them, or do you take your troubles to God? What does the example of Nehemiah teach you about how you should respond?

- Dr. Munroe said that every champion does not win every round, but if he perseveres, he wins the match. Have you just lost a "round"? How should you respond?

- Since prayer is where you receive the ability to continue the fight, are you finding time during the day to go to God with your fears, concerns, and spiritual weariness? What will you do to make time for prayer?

Acting on It

- Establish a daily prayer time with God.

- Read and meditate on John 15:4–8. Write down what these verses teach you about the nature of your God-given vision and what you need to do to fulfill it.

- Remind yourself of the importance of prayer by memorizing these verses:

By day the LORD directs his love, at night his song is with me—a prayer to the God of my life. (Psalm 42:8)

Be joyful in hope, patient in affliction, faithful in prayer. (Romans 12:12)

Pray in the Spirit on all occasions with all kinds of prayers and requests.

(Ephesians 6:18)

Praying about It

- In what ways are you relying on God for your life and vision? In what ways aren't you relying on Him? Be honest with God about how you are feeling. Then commit to Him the areas in which you aren't currently relying on Him. Praise Him for being your Strength and Help, and allow Him to encourage and refresh you through His sustaining presence.

- God will bring you through your difficulties and give you the victory through prayer based on His Word. When you face various problems and challenges, pray according to Scripture that addresses your need. Then, hold on to that Word in faith as you go about pursuing your vision.

PRAYER IS WHAT KEEPS YOU CONNECTED TO THE VISION-GIVER.

Notes

Writing Your Personal Vision Plan

This section of the study guide is designed to assist you in writing your personal vision plan. Read through chapter 17, "How to Write Your Personal Vision Plan," as well as "The Principles and Process of Vision" summaries and the "Keys to Fulfilling Your Vision" found on pages 223–24, 226 in *The Principles and Power of Vision*. Then use the spaces provided to answer the questions to the various steps, which you can use as guidelines for implementing your plan. Relevant page numbers in the book are listed for easy reference.

Step One: Eliminate Distractions (See page 218.)

Step Two: Find Your True Self

Write your personal purpose statement: (See pages 218–19.)

Step Three: Find Your True Vision

Write your personal vision statement: (See pages 219, 225–26.)

Activities:

Write your own legacy: (See pages 219–20, 225–26.)

Write your personal mission statement: (See pages 220, 225.)

Summarize your vision for your life in just one sentence: (See page 220.)

Step Four: Discover Your True Motivation

Answer the questions found on page 220:

Step Five: Identify Your Principles

Write out your life principles: (See pages 220–21.)

Step Six: Choose Your Goals and Objectives

Write out your goals: (See pages 221, 228–230.)

Write out your objectives: (See page 221.)

Step Seven: Identify Your Resources

Identify your human needs: (See pages 221, 227.)

Identify your resource needs: (See pages 222, 227.)

Write down your strengths: (See page 222.)

Write down your weaknesses: (See page 222.)

Step Eight: Commit to Your Vision (p. 222)

Write out a commitment to your vision here. When you have completed it, sign and date it.

Commit your vision to God, asking Him to clarify His purposes for you, refine your plans, and continue to lead you through the process.

Commit to the Lord whatever you do, and your plans will succeed.　　　(Proverbs 16:3)

GOD WILL DIRECT YOUR STEPS WHEN YOU MAKE A CONCRETE PLAN TO MOVE TOWARD WHAT YOU DESIRE.

Personal Planning and Goal-Setting Program

Year: _____

Name:_____

By God's grace, I commit to accomplishing the following goals this year:

Personal Spiritual Goals

1. _____

2. _____

3. _____

Personal Family Goals

1. _____

2. _____

3. _____

Personal Health Goals

1. _____

2. _____

3. _____

Personal Academic Goals

1. _____

2. _____

3. _____

Personal Career Goals

1. _____

2. _____

3. _____

Personal Relationship Goals

1. _____

2. _____

3. _____

Personal Financial Goals

1. _____

2. _____

3. _____

Personal Investment Goals

1. _____

2. _____

3. _____

Answer Key

Chapter One
Vision: The Key to Fulfilling Your Life's Purpose

1. Answers will vary.
2. Answers will vary.
3. dream
4. Without a vision of the future, life loses its meaning. An absence of meaning then leads to a lack of hope. Whenever people are hopeless about their life situations, they can become resentful of their jobs or families. They can feel as if they are wasting their lives, and they can start living with a vague but constant internal longing for something more. They may even stop participating in life in any significant way.
5. People rarely act on their ideas so that years go by and they still haven't done anything to develop or fulfill them.
6. has a dream but doesn't know how to bring it to pass
7. Some reasons a person will abandon or get sidetracked from his or her dream are: a lack of money; fulfilling the dream seems too time-consuming; other people are working against the person; the person's day job is making heavy demands; the person becomes discouraged because family members say the dream will never succeed.
8. design; vision
9. Fulfilling our visions brings purpose and meaning to our lives.
10. Dr. Munroe said that the very substance of life is for a person to find God's purpose and fulfill it.
11. Every human being was created to accomplish something specific that no one else can accomplish.
12. known; special
13. the passive force of ninety-nine people who are merely interested in doing or becoming something
14. Your gift will make a way for you in the world and enable you to fulfill your vision.
15. Answers may vary, but should include the following ideas: If education were the key to success, then everyone with higher education would be financially secure and happy. Someone who is intelligent or educated but isn't exercising or developing his gift is probably going to be poor, depressed, frustrated, and tired. Again, our gifts are the key to our success. They are what the world makes room for and will pay for.
16. You are responsible for stirring your gift up. You can do this by developing, refining, enhancing, and using it.

17. Although education can't give you your gift, it can help you to develop it so that it can be used to the maximum.

18. originals; imitators. You can avoid being an imitator by not trying to compete with or please everybody else, but instead deciding that you're going to find your own niche and make room for yourself in the world by using your gift.

19. False

20. A person can realize his dream by having a clear vision and acting on it. As long as a person can hold on to his vision, then there is always a chance for him to move out of his present circumstances and toward the fulfillment of his purpose.

21. (f) your understanding and practicing the principles of vision.

22. We are the sum total of the choices and decisions we make every day.

23. power; responsibility

Chapter Two
The Source of Vision

1. Answers will vary.

2. Vision always emanates from purpose. This is so because God is the Author of vision, and it is His nature to be purposeful in everything He does.

3. fulfill

4. right time; generation

5. God is eternal, and He lives in eternity. The vision He has put into your heart is also in His own heart. Therefore, your vision is "a piece of eternity" that He gave you to deliver in time and space—that is, on the earth during your lifetime. God has specifically placed you in time so that others on earth will be able to see a piece of eternity that is in Him.

6. God planned and established your purpose before you were born. In this sense, it has already been completed in eternity.

7. Instead of striving to fulfill what God has given you to do, you can rely on Him to finish it as you allow Him to guide you in the specifics of carrying it out.

8. Recognizing your purpose is knowing and understanding what you were born to accomplish. Having a vision is being able to see that purpose in your mind by faith and to begin to imagine it.

9. At its essence, vision is about God rather than about us. This is so because true vision isn't a human invention; rather, it's about the desires God imparts to us. It is the view of our future inspired by God; it is what He wants us to contribute in building His kingdom on earth.

10. The key to recognizing personal vision is understanding that God's will is as close to us as our most persistent thoughts and deepest desires.

11. God has placed His thoughts and desires into our hearts, and the will of God for us never changes.

12. One way to discern whether or not something is a vision from God is to determine whether you have a real desire (passion) to do it or merely a passing interest in it.

13. Another way to recognize true vision is when you persevere in your dream regardless of great obstacles.

14. unselfish. A real vision always focuses on helping humanity or building up others in some way.

15. Two things that indicate a person is pursuing selfish interests rather than true vision are (1) when a person is pursuing something at the expense of bringing turmoil and destruction to his family, and (2) when a person is pursuing wealth in order to fill his life with luxuries rather than using it as a resource to build God's kingdom.

16. compassion

17. A fourth way of knowing that a vision is real is when it is the only thing that gives you true satisfaction.

18. Many people don't recognize the vision God has placed within them because they don't have a vital connection with God.

19. A fifth key to understanding vision is to realize that it is both personal and corporate; personal vision will always be found within a larger corporate vision.

20. God doesn't give a vision to a group. He gives vision to an individual who shares his vision with a group and transfers it to them. The members of the group then run with the vision because they find in it a place for their own personal visions to be fulfilled.

21. cooperation

22. (c) stir up your personal vision.

23. You are a leader in the specific purpose God has given you to accomplish through your gift(s) because no one else but you can fulfill it.

24. Vision generates vision in that dreams always stir up other dreams. The leader of a corporate vision and all the participants in the vision stir up each other's individual dreams by sharing their visions and working harmoniously toward achieving the larger vision. When this happens, the divine deposit of destiny starts flowing, and visions become reality.

25. What will help you to keep stirring up your vision is to have people around you who believe in dreams that are even bigger than your own. Those with real vision are "people of understanding" who will cause your dream to rise from the deep well within you (see Proverbs 20:5) and will help you to make real progress toward your vision.

Chapter Three
Overcoming Obstacles to Vision

1. Answers will vary.
2. The first obstacle to fulfilling vision is not understanding the nature of vision.
3. specific
4. A mission is a general statement of purpose that declares the overall idea of what you want to accomplish. It is philosophical and abstract, not practical and concrete. In contrast, a vision is a very precise statement that has a specific emphasis and definable boundaries.
5. jealous; competition
6. We should measure the success of our visions by God's assignment to us and whether we are doing what He told us to do, rather than by what others are doing.
7. Another reason people aren't specific about their visions is that they're caught in a trap of wishful thinking; they never get beyond the dreaming stage of what they would like to do "someday."
8. wills; wishes. We do this by making concrete resolutions and taking specific steps to pursue our visions and goals.
9. A third reason people's visions never take specific shape is that they are perpetually indecisive—they can't make up their minds what they want to do in life.
10. (d) all of the above
11. A fourth reason people don't pursue specific visions is that they either make excuses for why they can't do what they know they should be doing or they never finish what they have started.
12. A fifth reason people don't focus on specific visions is that they fear their lives might not be well-balanced—that if they choose one thing they will miss out on what they really want to do or should be doing in life.
13. True balance is the maintenance of equilibrium while moving toward a destination.
14. A sixth reason people aren't specific about their visions is that they are trying to do too much.
15. Dr. Munroe realized that no one, including himself, was born or created to do everything.
16. certain; every
17. A seventh reason some people don't pursue specific visions is that they are multi-talented, and they don't know which of their talents or interests they should develop and use in life.
18. If you have many gifts and interests, you can pursue a specific vision by first guarding against the temptation to try to do everything. Next, no matter how many gifts

you have, don't let them distract you. You must decide to concentrate on one or two gifts and then stir them up. As you do, the other gifts will follow. God will not waste what He has given you.

19. The second obstacle to fulfilling vision is not recognizing the cost of accomplishing it.

20. diligence

21. If a person thinks he has had a string of bad luck in life or that he is an unlucky person, he will probably not make the effort necessary to make his vision succeed.

22. Some people don't recognize and pay the cost of vision because they blame outside forces for causing their visions to fail.

23. People blame (1) the actions or needs of other people and (2) their past experiences—educational, spiritual, social—or their past failures for preventing their visions from coming to pass.

24. No matter what your mistakes may have been or what your background may be, God still has a definite plan and purpose for your life. God is not finished until He's completed what He created you to be and do. Nothing you have done is so bad that it can compete with the forgiveness of Jesus. In addition, when God gives a gift, He doesn't change His mind regarding it. He is a restorer and a reclaimer. This means He will put back in you what life took out, so you can fulfill the vision He has given you.

25. When the winds of adversity blow in your life, your God-given vision will be your anchor.

26. The third obstacle to accomplishing vision is not knowing the principles for fulfilling it.

27. haphazardly. Successful visionaries operate according to established and time-tested principles that enable their visions to become reality.

Chapter Four
Principle #1:
Be Directed by a Clear Vision

1. Answers will vary.
2. Dr. Munroe said he discovered that the key to life is not only knowing what you are, but also why you are (your reason for existence). You should know your origin and purpose in God as well as your abilities and plans for the future.
3. If you are lazy or bored, it shows that you lack vision.
4. choose; decisive; faithful
5. Having a true work means doing what you were born to do. Having a job is a preliminary occupation that you do only until you are ready to fulfill your vision.

6. After your vision becomes clear to you, it will bother you deep inside, and you may become depressed, until you are able to take action on it.

7. One of the most significant questions you must answer for yourself is, "What is it that I want?"

8. The first thing you should do in answering this question is to ask God to confirm what He has put in your heart for you to do.

9. In order to find your vision, you must be in touch with the values and priorities of the kingdom of God.

10. lives on; possessions

11. Vision is a clear conception of something that is not yet reality, but which can exist. It is a strong image of a preferable future.

12. change

13. Sometimes, God will activate your vision when things are going well in order to stir up your life so that you will move forward and progress rather than become complacent. A vision will always take you from good to better and from better to best.

14. In living our lives, we shouldn't try to go back to the "good old days" because, if we do, we will not progress in what God has planned for us.

15. future; build on; return

16. The constant newness and change of vision keeps you fluid and mobile, ready to take the next step toward your purpose.

17. passion; moving forward

Chapter Five
Principle #2:
Know Your Potential for Fulfilling Vision

1. Answers will vary.

2. Your potential for fulfilling your vision is determined by the assignment God has given you to do.

3. equipped

4. ability; responsibility

5. God has put His vision and His Spirit within you.

6. (b) the power of God's Spirit working in you.

7. According to Ephesians 3:20, God will do *"immeasurably"* (NIV) or *"exceeding abundantly"* (KJV) beyond all you can ask or imagine.

8. It enabled Dr. Munroe to progress from the knowledge of his purpose to the faith that accompanies vision.

9. God gave you the gift of imagination to keep you from focusing only on your present conditions and to enable you to move forward with your vision.

10. You should be taking a "tour" of your vision in your imagination on a regular basis: Visit everything, check it out, see all the details, notice its value, and then come back to the present and say, "Let's go there, God!"

11. You shouldn't allow any other human being to judge your potential because others may not be able to see your purpose, and your abilities are determined by your purpose.

12. perfect

13. God gave you dreams to draw out what's already inside you and to activate His power in enabling you to achieve your vision.

14. God appoints, anoints, and distinguishes people because He doesn't like them to get lost in mediocrity; He wants their true selves (based on His purposes) to be revealed to the world.

15. The ability to accomplish your vision is manifested when you say yes to your dream and obey God.

16. Your present job might contain hidden potential for your true life's work. It might make a way for the resources you will need to fulfill your vision.

17. You should plant the seed of your vision by beginning to act on it and then nurture it by faith.

Chapter Six
Principle #3:
Develop a Concrete Plan for Your Vision

1. Answers will vary.
2. future
3. Dr. Munroe realized that if he didn't have a plan, God wouldn't have anything specific to direct him in.
4. Proverbs 16:1: *"To man belong the plans of the heart, but from the LORD comes the reply of the tongue."* Proverbs 16:9: *"In his heart a man plans his course, but the LORD determines his steps."*
5. When you receive an idea from God, you must soon cultivate it.
6. If you never work on your idea, it may go away, and God may give it to someone else to develop.
7. When you lack a plan, you will likely miss out on opportunities for fulfilling your vision.
8. on track
9. "Who am I?"
10. identity; God
11. "Where am I going?"

12. focus
13. A vision becomes a plan when it is captured, fleshed out, and written down.
14. God's part is to provide the explanation as to how the vision will be accomplished. He will explain how it can be paid for, who is going to work with it, and where the resources and facilities are going to come from.
15. God has given you a mind, the gift of imagination, the anointing of the Holy Spirit, and the vision of faith. He has also given you the ability to write so that you can put down on paper what you see in your heart.
16. Certain people won't be able to handle your plan while you're making it. Some people will try to talk you out of your plan, saying, "You can't do that!" If you listen to them, you will likely throw your plan away and give up on your vision.
17. Your dream is worth writing down because, if God gave it to you, it deserves to be done.
18. When Nehemiah gave credit to God for his vision and how it was coming to pass, he built up the faith of those who were going to work on the project.
19. prayers
20. fulfill

Chapter Seven
Principle #4:
Possess the Passion of Vision

1. Answers will vary.
2. Passionate people have discovered something more important than life itself.
3. false visions; ambition
4. One reason Dr. Munroe kept stressing the need for a clear guiding purpose in life is that vision is the precedent for passion.
5. When Paul gave a list of problems and tribulations as part of the proof that he was a genuine apostle, he was saying, in effect, "If the vision and assignment I received wasn't real, do you think I'd go through all those hardships?" He knew what his purpose in life was, and he was passionate about it. This is what kept him going through all his struggles.
6. Faithfulness
7. If you're going to go after your vision, you can expect to experience resistance.
8. passion; feed
9. It shows that you aren't passionate about your vision.
10. Many people fail to win at pursuing their visions because they give up when they fall down the first time. They stop too soon.

11. No matter how tough things are, a passionate person's perspective is, "What I believe is bigger than what I see."
12. eager
13. Passion is willing to pay the price to fulfill the vision.
14. focused
15. defy the odds; fulfillment

Chapter Eight
Principle #5:
Develop the Faith of Vision

1. Answers will vary.
2. Sight is a function of the eyes, while vision is a function of the heart.
3. believes
4. You are to walk according to what is in your heart; you are to let what is in your heart dictate how you see life.
5. faith
6. Hebrews 11:1 says that *"faith is the substance of things hoped for, the evidence of things not seen* [that you cannot see]" (NKJV).
7. Dr. Munroe defined faith as vision in the heart. He said that faith is seeing the future in the present.
8. Sight without vision is dangerous because it has no hope. It sees only present problems and challenges and not things as they could be.
9. environment
10. You were designed to operate as God operates.
11. God functions in faith by having an idea, visualizing it, and then creating it by speaking His thoughts into being.
12. important; powerful
13. When you speak words expressing what you see in your vision, your words become creative power to help bring that vision to fruition.
14. You can undermine your vision by continually thinking and declaring negative things about yourself.
15. Faith sees problems as opportunities for ministry, service, or business.
16. (b) think and expect great things.
17. Ideas
18. it can live beyond the grave
19. The faith of vision is crucial because the way you see things determines how you think and act and, therefore, whether or not your vision will become reality.

Chapter Nine
Principle #6:
Understand the Process of Vision

1. Answers will vary.
2. Answers will vary.
3. God usually brings to pass His plans for our lives in a gradual way.
4. God will rarely tell you exactly how He will take you to the completion of your vision.
5. ready
6. The process God is taking you through to arrive at your destination is designed to prepare you to receive and work in your vision.
7. The process of vision will develop your character and produce responsibility in you.
8. If God were to tell you exactly what is going to happen as you progress toward your vision, you might refuse the vision because of the various learning experiences, challenges, and hardships you will need to go through before you are ready for your vision.
9. good reason
10. perfect plan
11. When we go through difficult times, we often think that God has stopped working to fulfill our purposes. However, our purposes are still coming; again, God is preparing us for them.
12. God is trying to work out of us attitudes of complaint and lack of faith so that they won't hinder us in our visions.
13. qualified
14. Your vision will culminate in God's timing.
15. While you have the job, you should submit yourself to it, learn what you're supposed to learn, and get all the knowledge that you can from it, because God is using it to prepare you for your life's work.
16. Purpose gives meaning to your present job; it enables you to keep moving forward during this training period because you know you're preparing for your true work.
17. As you wait for your dream, you must live by faith and inner vision, not by what you see.

Chapter Ten
Principle #7:
Set the Priorities of Vision

1. Answers will vary.

2. Understanding priority will help you to accomplish your dream because priority is the key to effective decision-making.
3. Your choices and preferences reveal who you are and what you value in life.
4. Dr. Munroe says that what you have decided for the last fifteen, twenty, or thirty years of your life has significantly contributed to who you are today.
5. You can tell (for the most part) the kind of life you're going to have in the future by the decisions you are making today.
6. *yes; no*
7. When people don't succeed in their visions, it is often because they don't understand that prioritizing creates useful limits on their choices.
8. True
9. You determine what is beneficial to you based on the needs of your vision. Something is beneficial if it relates to what you want to accomplish and takes you to your goal.
10. best
11. You might keep drifting off in the wrong direction if you have your own ideas about what you want to do for God instead of consulting Him about what He wants and then doing what He has specifically told you to do.
12. If you keep taking your eyes off the mark (your vision), and if you allow yourself to be pulled in many different directions by all kinds of distractions, then you will end up in a place where you don't really want to be.
13. You can make sure you will hit the mark by joining with God's plan for your life and letting His yoke guide you.
14. People sometimes become involved in too many things because they're trying to impress God and other people by showing them how much they are capable of doing.
15. disciplined
16. If you are afraid to take decisive action to move toward your vision, this should be your perspective: It is better to make a decision that will prove to be wrong, but which you can learn from, than not to make any decision at all and never learn anything.
17. People who succeed try. People who don't try have no chance of success.

Chapter Eleven
Principle #8:
Recognize People's Influence on Vision

1. Answers will vary.
2. You need other people if you are going to be successful in life because you were not created to fulfill your vision alone. Again, individual purpose is always fulfilled within a larger or corporate purpose.

3. positive
4. If you have no dream, or if you do not begin to act on it, the people who are supposed to help you won't know where to find you (and therefore won't be able to help you).
5. When you begin to act on your vision, it will stir up both those who want to help you and those who want to hinder you.
6. The law of association states that you become like those with whom you spend time.
7. powerful; subtle
8. People have the potential to create your environment.
9. mind-set; future
10. You should generally choose friends who are going in the same direction you are and who want to obtain the same things you do, so you can reinforce one another.
11. As you progress toward your vision, you should be asking yourself these three questions: (1) "With whom am I spending time?" (2) "What are these people doing to me?" (3) "Is what other people are doing to me a good thing in relation to my vision?"
12. Certain people may become angry with you or even begin to hate you when you step out and do something they have never done because they don't want to feel left behind or because you are exposing their own lack of vision.
13. Sometimes, the people who can be the most detrimental to the fulfillment of your vision are the members of your own family. This is because they have lived with you for such a long time that they think they know who you are (your abilities and limitations), so they try to talk you out of all your dreams.
14. other people's expectations
15. When people oppose you and your vision, you need to keep your eyes on the mark, continue working, and keep on building; keep moving forward with your vision.
16. Three things you can do to protect your vision are disassociation, limited association, and expanded association.
17. You should disassociate yourself from people who aren't going anywhere and don't want to go anywhere in life.
18. There are some people you should just be acquainted with so that you can back off from them if being with them causes your vision to falter.
19. You can protect your mental environment by spending major time with positive influence and minor time with negative influence.
20. You should expand your association with people who have the same philosophy and discipline that you do, who exhibit the kind of character that you want to have, and who are people of vision.

Chapter Twelve
Principle #9:
Employ the Provision of Vision

1. Answers will vary.
2. True
3. It is your job to understand, believe, and write down your vision while it is God's responsibility to explain how He's going to accomplish it in His own time.
4. This arrangement frees you to be creative and productive in pursuing your vision.
5. God often gives us dreams that confound us at first because He wants to make sure we don't attempt to fulfill them apart from Him. If we try to do so, we won't succeed, because the resources won't be available.
6. God manifests the provision when you act on your vision.
7. attracts
8. God has already blessed you with every spiritual blessing in the heavenly places, with everything you need to fulfill your vision.
9. The first misconception of prosperity is prosperity as excess or hoarding. The second is prosperity as future needs met today.
10. today's
11. True prosperity means to be free of worry and fear and reflects a state of contentedness that everything necessary is being taken care of.
12. prosperity; built-in
13. The nature and degree of your prosperity is determined by what your assignment is.
14. Sometimes, God doesn't give us all the resources we need to fulfill our visions because He has called other people to provide them for us.
15. Obedience to your vision is not just a private issue because your vision affects not only your life, but also the lives of everyone who is supposed to work with you and be impacted by your life.
16. If we are pursuing the wrong assignments (visions), there are some things God can't supply us with because the provision isn't there unless the visions are ours. God can't give us what doesn't belong to us. Again, knowing God's will for our lives is the key to our prosperity.
17. The first way God provides for our visions is through our ability to obtain and use land and the resources (wealth) inherent in it.
18. You will likely need to exercise discipline and self-control in your life by controlling your spending, avoiding waste, cutting back on your expenses, and saving money so that you can save up a down payment to buy property.
19. The second way God provides for our visions is through our ability to work.

20. Dr. Munroe defined work as the passion that is generated by a purpose.
21. potential
22. The third way God provides for our visions is through the ability He has given us to cultivate things.
23. A large part of the gift of cultivation is the ability to see potential in what others view as wasteland.
24. preserve; reserve
25. The fifth way God provides for vision is through our ability to pass along wealth— through enabling us to help future generations with their dreams.

Chapter Thirteen
Principle #10:
Use Persistence in Achieving the Vision

1. Answers will vary.
2. Having faithfulness in regard to your vision means being true to what you have decided to accomplish and letting nothing stop you.
3. To be steadfast means to stand fast or stand steady in the face of resistance.
4. Opposition should strengthen your resolve, revive your stamina, and make you wiser.
5. stand up; fear
6. The first challenge or pressure we may experience in life is a difficult family background.
7. Your relationship with your Father in heaven will help you overcome a difficult background and fulfill your purpose as God's child.
8. The second challenge or pressure we may experience in life is family expectations.
9. As difficult as it might be to experience the disapproval of your family members, you must follow the vision God has given you. At the same time, you should show love and respect to your family.
10. The third challenge or pressure we may experience in life is the jealousy and scheming of others.
11. You can overcome such opposition when the vision in your heart is larger than what is coming against you, so that you persist in your life's purpose.
12. diligence
13. When it comes to their visions, persistent people win because they never take no for an answer.
14. According to Dr. Munroe, the light of God's vision in your heart is so strong and bright that all the darkness of the planet, all the darkness of people's opinions, and all the darkness of past failures can never put it out.

15. *Perseverance* means "to bear up under pressure."
16. Character
17. In order to draw the fragrance of His glory from your life, God will allow you to be put under stress. The purpose of this pressure is to get rid of what is not of God and to leave what is pure gold.
18. When you understand that pressure is good for you, there will be no stopping you because pressure is one of the keys to perseverance.
19. (a) endure to the end.
20. authenticity
21. A crisis can be a turning point at which our understanding of and commitment to the vision is tested and matured. A crisis can lead you to greater challenge and victory.

Chapter Fourteen
Principle #11:
Be Patient in the Fulfillment of Vision

1. Answers will vary.
2. Answers will vary.
3. The result of your having patience or persevering is that you will receive what God has promised. You must also have confidence (faith) and do the will of God to receive this result.
4. ensures
5. When some people make plans to carry out their visions, they try to force those plans into their own timetable or their own way of bringing them to pass. This is counter-productive because you cannot rush a vision. It is given by God, and He will carry it out in His own time.
6. You need to patiently rely on God's guidance every step of the way because you are not all-knowing, as He is. You don't know what is best for your vision.
7. Your vision will come to pass at just the right time/in the fullness of time.
8. (d) anticipation
9. pace
10. When you are patient in the fulfillment of your vision, you are able to be calm and at peace in the midst of uncertainty.
11. You can endure the "cross" of life's difficulties while waiting for your vision by seeing the joy of the end (fulfillment) of your vision. (See Hebrews 12:2.)
12. time; change
13. Patience is the key to power over adversity and turmoil.
14. Patience is more powerful than might in a person because someone who is patient does not react to provocation. His waiting eventually unnerves and overcomes the opposition.

15. According to James 1:3 (NKJV), the testing of our faith produces patience.
16. According to James 1:4 (NKJV), patience perfects and completes us so that we lack nothing for the fulfillment of our purposes in God.

Chapter Fifteen
Principle #12:
Stay Connected to the Source of Vision

1. Answers will vary.
2. Author; Support
3. Apart from God, you can accomplish nothing of His purpose.
4. If you stay in touch with God, you will always be nourished in both life and vision.
5. demands
6. God will bring you through your difficulties and give you the victory through prayer based on His Word.
7. God will encourage and refresh you so that you can continue to pursue your vision.
8. fight
9. It is crucial for you to find times during the day when you can go before God with your fears and receive the reassurance that He is with you.
10. resource
11. When people attack your dream, you should go to God and trust in His deliverance, as Nehemiah did. Stay connected to your Source for the renewal of your purpose, faith, and strength, and you will be able to persevere to victory.
12. You shouldn't try to explain and give an answer for everything because you can't explain anything to critics. Their motives are already contaminated, and they'll use your words against you.
13. You can be assured that He will bring your vision to pass.

About the Author

Dr. Myles Munroe (1954–2014) was an international motivational speaker, best-selling author, educator, leadership mentor, and consultant for government and business. Traveling extensively throughout the world, Dr. Munroe addressed critical issues affecting the full range of human, social, and spiritual development. The central theme of his message is the maximization of individual potential, including the transformation of followers into leaders and leaders into agents of change.

Dr. Munroe was founder and president of Bahamas Faith Ministries International (BFMI), a multidimensional organization headquartered in Nassau, Bahamas. He was chief executive officer and chairman of the board of the International Third World Leaders Association and president of the International Leadership Training Institute.

Dr. Munroe was also the founder and executive producer of a number of radio and television programs aired worldwide. In addition, he was a frequent guest on other television and radio programs and international networks and was a contributing writer for various Bible editions, journals, magazines, and newsletters, such as *The Believer's Topical Bible, The African Cultural Heritage Topical Bible, Charisma Life Christian Magazine,* and *Ministries Today.* He was a popular author of more than forty books, including *The Power of Character in Leadership, The Purpose and Power of Authority, The Principles and Benefits of Change, Becoming a Leader, The Purpose and Power of the Holy Spirit, The Spirit of Leadership, The Principles and Power of Vision, Understanding the Purpose and Power of Prayer, Understanding the Purpose and Power of Women,* and *Understanding the Purpose and Power of Men.* Dr. Munroe has changed the lives of multitudes around the world with a powerful message that inspires, motivates, challenges, and empowers people to discover personal purpose, develop true potential, and manifest their unique leadership abilities. For over thirty years, he trained tens of thousands of leaders in business, industry, education, government, and religion. He personally addressed over 500,000 people each year on personal and professional development. His appeal and message transcend age, race, culture, creed, and economic background.

Dr. Munroe earned B.A. and M.A. degrees from Oral Roberts University and the University of Tulsa, and was awarded a number of honorary doctoral degrees. He also served as an adjunct professor of the Graduate School of Theology at Oral Roberts University.

The parents of two adult children, Charisa and Chairo (Myles Jr.), Dr. Munroe and his wife, Ruth, traveled as a team and were involved in teaching seminars together. Both were leaders who ministered with sensitive hearts and international vision. In November 2014, they were tragically killed in an airplane crash en route to an annual leadership conference sponsored by Bahamas Faith Ministries International. A statement from Dr. Munroe in his book *The Power of Character in Leadership* summarizes his own legacy: "Remember that character ensures the longevity of leadership, and men and women of principle will leave important legacies and be remembered by future generations."